Giganotosaurus/ Giganotosaurio

by Joanne Mattern

Illustrations by Jeffrey Mangiat

Reading consultant: Susan Nations, M.Ed., author, literacy coach, consultant in literacy development

Science consultant: Philip J. Currie, Ph.D., Professor and Canada Research Chair of Dinosaur Palaeobiology at the University of Alberta, Canada

WEEKLY READER®
PUBLISHING

Please visit our web site at: www.garethstevens.com
For a free color catalog describing ourlist of high-quality books,
call 1-800-542-2595 (USA) or 1-800-387-3178 (Canada).
Our fax: 1-877-542-2596.

Library of Congress Cataloging-in-Publication Data available upon request from publisher.
Fax (414) 336-0157 for the attention of the Publishing Records Department.

ISBN-13: 978-0-8368-8019-9 (lib. bdg.)
ISBN-13: 978-0-8368-8026-7 (softcover)

This edition first published in 2007 by
Weekly Reader® Books
An Imprint of Gareth Stevens Publishing
1 Reader's Digest Road
Pleasantville, NY 10570-7000 USA

Copyright © 2007 by Weekly Reader® Early Learning Library

Managing editor: Valerie J. Weber
Art direction, cover and layout design: Tammy West
Spanish translation: Tatiana Acosta and Guillermo Gutiérrez

Printed in the United States of America

2 3 4 5 6 7 8 9 10 10 09

Note to Educators and Parents

Reading is such an exciting adventure for young children! They are beginning to integrate their oral language skills with written language. To encourage children along the path to early literacy, books must be colorful, engaging, and interesting; they should invite the young reader to explore both the print and the pictures.

Let's Read about Dinosaurs is a new series designed to help children read about some of their favorite — and most fearsome — animals. In each book, young readers will learn how each dinosaur survived so long ago.

Each book is specially designed to support the young reader in the reading process. The familiar topics are appealing to young children and invite them to read — and re-read — again and again. The full-color photographs and enhanced text further support the student during the reading process.

In addition to serving as wonderful picture books in schools, libraries, homes, and other places where children learn to love reading, these books are specifically intended to be read within an instructional guided reading group. This small group setting allows beginning readers to work with a fluent adult model as they make meaning from the text. After children develop fluency with the text and content, the book can be read independently. Children and adults alike will find these books supportive, engaging, and fun!

— Susan Nations, M.Ed., author, literacy coach, and consultant in literacy development

Nota para los maestros y los padres

¡Leer es una aventura tan emocionante para los niños pequeños! A esta edad están comenzando a integrar su manejo del lenguaje oral con el lenguaje escrito. Para animar a los niños en el camino de la lectura incipiente, los libros deben ser coloridos, estimulantes e interesantes; deben invitar a los jóvenes lectores a explorar la letra impresa y las ilustraciones.

Conozcamos a los dinosaurios es una nueva colección diseñada para presentar a los niños información sobre algunos de sus animales favoritos — y más temibles. En cada libro, los jóvenes lectores aprenderán cómo sobrevivió hace tanto tiempo un dinosaurio.

Cada libro está especialmente diseñado para ayudar a los jóvenes lectores en el proceso de lectura. Los temas familiares llaman la atención de los niños y los invitan a leer una y otra vez. Las fotografías a todo color y el tamaño de la letra ayudan aún más al estudiante en el proceso de lectura.

Además de servir como maravillosos libros ilustrados en escuelas, bibliotecas, hogares y otros lugares donde los niños aprenden a amar la lectura, estos libros han sido especialmente concebidos para ser leídos en un grupo de lectura guiada. Este contexto permite que los lectores incipientes trabajen con un adulto que domina la lectura mientras van determinando el significado del texto. Una vez que los niños dominan el texto y el contenido, el libro puede ser leído de manera independiente. ¡Estos libros les resultarán útiles, estimulantes y divertidos a niños y a adultos por igual!

— Susan Nations, M.Ed., autora, tutora de alfabetización y consultora de desarrollo de la lectura

Look at this big dinosaur! Its name is Giganotosaurus.

¡Mira este enorme dinosaurio! Es un giganotosaurio.

5

Giganotosaurus was about as long as three minivans. Giganotosaurus weighed as much as four cars. It was as tall as two men.

-- -- -- -- -- -- -- -- -- -- -- -- -- -- --

El giganotosaurio era tan largo como tres camionetas. Pesaba tanto como cuatro autos. Era tan alto como dos hombres.

Giganotosaurus was a fierce hunter! Its good sense of smell helped it find other dinosaurs to eat.

-- -- -- -- -- -- -- -- -- -- -- -- -- --

¡El giganotosaurio era un fiero cazador! Su buen sentido del olfato lo ayudaba a encontrar a otros dinosaurios para comérselos.

Giganotosaurus could run fast. Its speed also helped it catch other dinosaurs to eat.

El giganotosaurio podía correr muy rápido. Su velocidad también lo ayudaba a cazar a otros dinosaurios para comérselos.

Long, sharp teeth lined
its big jaws. They helped
Giganotosaurus bite and eat
other animals.

- - - - - - - - - - - - - -

Sus grandes mandíbulas
estaban llenas de dientes
largos y afilados. Estos dientes
permitían al giganotosaurio
morder y devorar a otros
animales.

13

Giganotosaurus had long back legs. Its arms were short! Look at the sharp **claws** on its fingers and toes.

El giganotosaurio tenía unas largas patas traseras. ¡Sus brazos eran cortos! Mira las afiladas **garras** que tiene en los dedos.

arms/brazos

claws/garras

15

Scientists think Giganotosaurus may have hunted in packs. Lots of Giganotosaurus could kill a bigger dinosaur.

— — — — — — — — — — — — — —

Los científicos piensan que el giganotosaurio cazaba en grupos. Muchos giganotosaurios podían matar a un dinosaurio más grande.

Scientists did not know about Giganotosaurus until 1994. Then scientists found this dinosaur's bones.

Hasta 1994, los científicos no sabían que había existido el giganotosaurio. Entonces fue cuando descubrieron los huesos de este dinosaurio.

Today scientists are looking for more Giganotosaurus fossils. They hope studying this dinosaur will tell us more about the past.

━ ━ ━ ━ ━ ━ ━ ━ ━ ━ ━ ━ ━ ━ ━

Los científicos están buscando más fósiles de giganotosaurio. Tienen la esperanza de que estudiar a este dinosaurio nos ayudará a entender mejor el pasado.

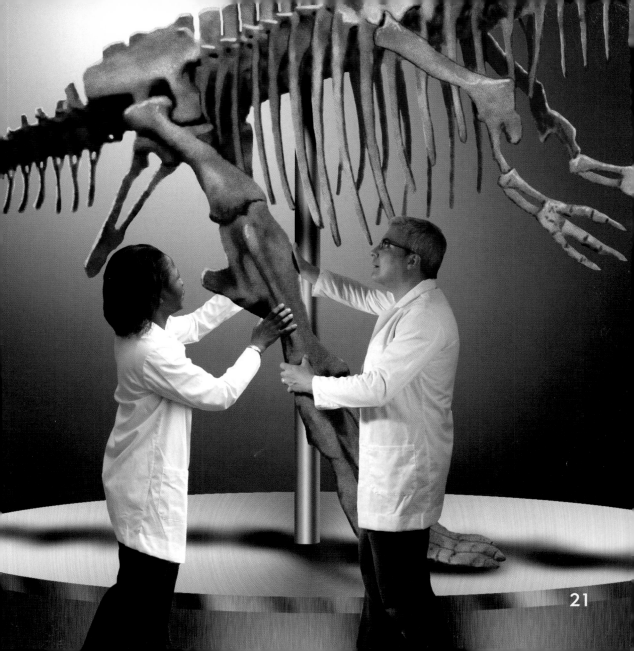

Glossary

fierce — strong and dangerous
fossils — bones or remains of animals and
plants that died a long time ago
Giganotosaurus — a huge, meat-eating dinosaur.
You say its name like this: jig-a-NOTE-o-SAW-rus.
scientists — people who study nature

Glosario

científicos — personas que estudian la naturaleza
fiero — fuerte y peligroso
fósiles — huesos o restos de animales y plantas
que murieron hace mucho tiempo
giganotosaurio — dinosaurio carnívoro de gran tamaño

For More Information/ Más información

Books/Libros

Dinosaurs Big and Small. Let's-Read-and-Find-Out Science (series). Kathleen Weidner Zoehfeld (HarperTrophy)

Dinosaurs! The Biggest Baddest Strangest Fastest. Howard Zimmerman (Atheneum)

Giganotosaurus and Other Big Dinosaurs. Dougal Dixon (Picture Window Books)

New Dinos: The Latest Finds! The Coolest Dinosaur Discoveries! Shelley Tanaka (Atheneum)

Index/Índice

About the Author

Joanne Mattern has written more than 150 books for children. She has written about weird animals, sports, world cities, dinosaurs, and many other subjects. Joanne also works in her local library. She lives in New York State with her husband, three daughters, and assorted pets. She enjoys animals, music, going to baseball games, reading, and visiting schools to talk about her books.

Información sobre la autora

Joanne Mattern ha escrito más de ciento cincuenta libros para niños. Ha escrito textos sobre animales extraños, deportes, ciudades del mundo, dinosaurios y muchos otros temas. Además, Joanne trabaja en la biblioteca de su comunidad. Vive en el estado de Nueva York con su esposo, sus tres hijas y varias mascotas. A Joanne le gustan los animales, la música, ir al béisbol, leer y hacer visitas a las escuelas para hablar de sus libros.